MAD ABOUT
MONEY

ALISON HAWES

FULL FLIGHT

Coleg Cambria

79044

COLEG CAMBRIA DEESIDE
LIBRARY

CLASS No. F HAW

ACCESS No. 79044

D1354410

Badger Publishing Limited
Oldmedow Road,
Hardwick Industrial Estate,
King's Lynn PE30 4JJ
Telephone: 01438 791037

www.badgerlearning.co.uk

2 4 6 8 10 9 7 5 3 1

Mad About Money ISBN 978-1-84424-846-9 (second edition) 2013

Publisher: Susan Ross
Senior Editor: Danny Pearson
Designer: Fiona Grant

Photos: Cover image: OJO Images / Rex Features
Illustrations: Laszlo Veres and Ian West
Page 4: Ann Pickford / Rex Features
Page 5: Image Source / Rex Features
Page 7: Petar Petrov/AP/Press Association Images
Page 8: reproduced by courtesy of the Royal Mint
Page 12: Ben Molyneux/Eye Ubiquitous/Press Association Images
Page 13: David Cheskin/PA Archive/Press Association Images
Page 16: Elise Amendola/AP/Press Association Images
Page 17: ALAMY
Page 24: TUNO DE VIEIRA/AP/Press Association Images
Page 25: Uli Deck/DPA/Press Association Images
Page 26: Laura Cioccarelli/Milestone/Empics Entertainment
Page 27: ALAMY
Page 30: Rex Features

Attempts to contact all copyright holders have been made.
If any omitted would care to contact Badger Learning, we will be
happy to make appropriate arrangements.

Contents

1.	The first money	4
2.	Metal money	6
3.	Paper money	10
4.	Plastic money	15
5.	Pocket money	18
6.	Fake money	20
7.	Stolen money	22
8.	Loads of money!	26
Index		32

1. THE FIRST MONEY

When we think of money we think of coins, cards and notes.

But in the past there were none of these. So people had to use other things instead.

All these items have been used as money in the past. They were all things that were valuable to people at the time.

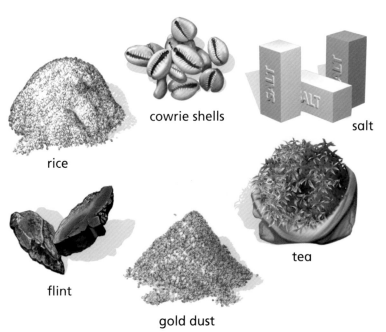

cowrie shells

salt

rice

tea

flint

gold dust

MONEY BOX FACT
Long ago in Sumatra, people used skulls as money!

2. METAL MONEY

Eventually, people began to use bits of metal or metal rings as money.

This led to the first coins being made.

The first coins were made about 2,600 years ago in Turkey.

They were made from a mixture of silver and gold.

Coins were easy to carry around and lasted for a long time, so they became very popular.

The very first coins were made by hand.

MONEY BOX FACT
Some coins were made with holes in them. Coins like this could be kept on a string.

The coins we use today in the UK are made at the Royal Mint in Wales.

The Royal Mint has been making coins for about 1,000 years.

It makes coins for the UK and for at least 60 different countries too!

MONEY BOX FACT
The Royal Mint can make 700 coins a minute!

Coins are now made by machine rather than by hand.

Machines roll metal into thin strips and stamp out blank coins.

Then another machine stamps each coin with the correct design.

MONEY BOX FACT
Jersey, Guernsey and the Isle of Man have different coins from the rest of the UK.

3. PAPER MONEY

The first paper money was made in China over 1,000 years ago.

This is one of the oldest notes that still exists. It comes from China. It is over 600 years old.

The biggest bank note ever produced in the world was as big as a comic. Just a thousand of them were made.

> **MONEY BOX FACT**
> The smallest note ever made was as small as a stamp.

Paper money was not made in the UK
until about 300 years ago.

The first bank notes were written by
hand on bank paper.

Now bank notes are printed on big sheets.

MONEY BOX FACT
Today, paper money is not made
from paper. It is made from cotton.

In England and Wales today, there are £5, £10, £20 and £50 notes.

There used to be £1 notes, like this:

But now we use £1 and £2 coins instead, as they last longer than the old £1 notes.

As paper money does not last very long, old notes are destroyed and new ones are printed every year.

In 2012/2013, the Bank of England destroyed more than 845 million old notes and printed 1,310 million new ones.

MONEY BOX FACT
In 2012, £13,384 of Bank of England bank notes were accidentally washed, chewed, torn or damaged.

Look at a bank note, like this one:

Can you see the
hologram here?

Can you feel the
words here?

Can you see the
metal strip here?

Can you see the
Queen here?

Things like this on a bank note make it
difficult for people to make fake notes.

MONEY BOX FACT
The strip in some notes
is now made of plastic.

4. PLASTIC MONEY

In some countries, like Australia, 'paper money' is now made of plastic.

Plastic notes are a good idea as they do not rip or get wet. So they last about four times longer than paper ones.

Today, you can pay for things with cash or you can pay with plastic cards!

Some plastic bank cards and plastic credit cards are CHIP and PIN cards.

The CHIP is the little computer chip in the card.

The PIN is the number you need to use the card.

Plastic cards can be used to pay for things
on the internet and the phone, too.

Bank cards can also be used to get
cash out of the bank.

5. POCKET MONEY

Do you get pocket money? How much do you get and what do you spend it on?

This is what a bank found out about pocket money in the UK in 2012:

1) Most 8 to 15 year olds get pocket money.
2) Boys get more pocket money than girls!
3) Just less than half of boys and girls think they should get more pocket money!

4) Most children save some of their pocket money.
5) Children in London get the most pocket money in the UK.
6) The average pocket money for 8 to 15 year olds is £5.98 a week.

(Source: Halifax Pocket Money Survey 2012)

6. FAKE MONEY

Some of the most convincing forged
money ever made was made in the UK
in the 1990s.

It was made by a man called Stephen Jory. He printed £50 million in fake £20 notes. But Stephen was eventually caught and sent to prison.

But his fake money was so convincing, the Bank of England had to change the design of the £20 note!

Albert Talton was America's biggest forger of fake money. He made $7 million in fake US hundred dollar bills.

Eventually, some of his fake bills were spotted and he was arrested in 2008. He was sent to prison for nine years.

7. STOLEN MONEY

In the UK, in 1963, a gang of men stole £2.6 million from a train. The gang was sent to prison, but some of them escaped!

Most of the money from the robbery has never been found.

MONEY BOX FACT
One of the train robbers escaped from prison. He was on the run for 35 years. Then he went back to prison!

The largest cash robbery in British history took place in Kent in 2006. A gang of robbers kidnapped the manager of the depot where the money was kept. They also kidnapped his family.

They were all taken to the depot where they and the depot staff were held while the robbery took place.

Before they left with £53 million, the robbers locked the staff into cash cages. The staff eventually escaped and called the police.

By 2010, all but one member of the gang were behind bars.

MONEY BOX FACT
Half of all bank robberies happen on a Friday!

One of the biggest bank robberies in the world was in Brazil in 2005.

A gang of robbers dug a tunnel 80 metres long to get into the bank.

It took several months for the gang to plan the robbery and dig the tunnel under the bank from a nearby building. They stole over $70 million.

In 1983, six men set out to rob £3 million in cash from a warehouse at Heathrow Airport.

But when they got there they found three tonnes of gold! They escaped with £26 million in gold, diamonds and cash. Most of the gold has never been found and only two of the gang are in prison.

8. *LOADS OF MONEY!*

One of the richest people in the world is
Bill Gates.

He makes his money from computers.
But he is not a millionaire. He is a billionaire!

He uses billions of dollars of his money to
help people with malaria and other illnesses.

In 2013, there were 1,426 billionaires in the world.

Twenty–nine of them were under 40 years old. The youngest billionaires in the world are Mark Zuckerberg and Dustin Moskovitz. They created Facebook

MONEY BOX FACT
The richest country in the world is Qatar. It is also one of the smallest countries in the world.

In the USA, a woman used a stolen credit card in a shop.

When the shopkeeper looked at the card, she was very surprised.

It was *her* credit card!

She rang the police and ran after the woman.

In 2005 a robber stole money from a shop.

He did not keep the money for himself. He gave it away.

But the police still got him.

Some people try to win lots of money by playing the lottery.

Most people who play the lottery do not win. But a tiny number of people win millions!

Just think what would happen if you won £1 million.

What would you do with all that money?

INDEX

bank 17, 18, 24
bank notes
10, 11, 13, 14
Bank of England 13, 21
billionaire 26, 27
CHIP 16
coins 4, 6, 7, 8, 9, 12
cowrie shells 5
credit cards 4, 16, 17, 28
fake 14, 20, 21
flint 5
forged 20, 21
Gates, Bill 26
gold 7, 25
gold dust 5
hologram 14

lottery 30
metal strip 14
millionaire 26
Moskovitz, Dustin 27
PIN 16
pocket money 18, 19
rice 5
richest 26, 27
robbery, bank 23, 24
robbery, train 22
Royal Mint 8
salt 5
silver 7
skulls 5
tea 5
Zuckerberg, Mark 27